Dead,

Dinner,

or Naked

Dead,

Dinner,

or Naked

Poems by
Evan Zimroth

TriQuarterly Books
Northwestern University Press

Designed by Gini Kondziolka

For information, contact:
TriQuarterly Books
Northwestern University
2020 Ridge Avenue
Evanston, IL 60208-4302

Library of Congress Catalog Card Number: 92-62257

ISBN 0-916384-10-1 (cloth)
ISBN 0-916384-14-4 (paper)

TriQuarterly Books
Northwestern University Press

Acknowledgments

Poetry: "Postcard From Idyllic Isle la Motte," "Front Porch," "Another Trashy Aubade," "On Hearing That Childbirth Is Like Orgasm," "Unfinished Portraits," "Lilly's Song"

Pequod: "Wintering," "The Faith-Healer," "Square Laurent Prache"

The Atlantic: "City Blizzard"

Women's Studies: "Ode After Nelly Sachs," "Planting Children: 1939"

The Hudson Review: "Morning Coffee on Isle la Motte"

5 A.M.: "Photo," "Do You Take"

The Little Magazine: "Breathing," "Just Another Love Affair," "Each Summer," "Café"

Woodstock Poetry Review: "In Heat"

Denver Quarterly: "She Wakes Up"

Tikkun: "Dead, Dinner, or Naked," "Nervus Erotis"

The Ledge: "Sakura Park" ["The Park, at Midnight"], "Burn," "What He Knew"

The following poems are in anthologies:

"Lilly's Song," *The Yearbook of American Poetry: 1981*

"Planting Children: 1939," *My Country Is the Whole World* (Routledge & Kegan Paul, 1983)

"Planting Children: 1939," "Front Porch," *Early Ripening: American Women's Poetry Now*, ed. Marge Piercy (Pandora Press, 1987)

"Planting Children: 1939," "Breathing," *In the Gold of Flesh: Poems of Birth & Motherhood*, ed. Rosemary Palmeira (The Women's Press Ltd., 1990)

"Dead, Dinner, or Naked," *Tikkun Anthology* (Tikkun Books, 1992)

I wish to thank the New York Foundation for the Arts for a Fellowship Award in Poetry, 1985-86, and the City University of New York for a PSC-CUNY Creative Writing Award in Poetry, 1990. Grateful thanks also to Lawrence Joseph.

Also by Evan Zimroth

Giselle Considers Her Future (1978)

for my father
in memory of my mother
▼

Contents

III

I

▼

Café

Now, at last, I see why, relentlessly,
we meet in restaurants. Because
it's funny to be forty, married,
mired in one's children, and so ferociously
attuned, so full of fantasy,
that I visit each innocuous
surrender with a charge. Coffee? Sure.
I read: Bed? Why, certainly.
Your place or mine? I used to think
that any man who beckoned
I would follow, but now I know
I'm more ambivalent. You might say,
more scared. Talk, and in a public spot,
will do as well as sex, and talk
we can be seen at. It's like a drug
I take to immunize myself
against disease: over coffee
my fever is abrupt, authentic, quickly starved.

Unfinished Portraits

1.

Her scarf is knotted loosely
under her collar; the small gold hoops
threading her ears pick up
the sun as it jangles into the room.
If she were alone, you would
not join her, for her eyes
are in trust—yet she lures
like squandering gold. Oh

the investments she's made, the suffering:
everyone says how she's suffered, how her heart
closed some far-back day, and how little
she would eat. They had to come at her with needles.
When she married the lawyer, finally,
she shrugged it off.
Another day, another debit.

2.

Everything secure: bangs cut
firmly, circle-pin
glinting at her throat, saying
Untouched, untouched. Only her poems

are stained, and the husband
moving his furniture
as if she were a leper. He tells his friends
he needs a little bouncy-bouncy
now and then; he says her linen-closet
drives him crazy. Both know
their time is up. She nibbles
her *thesaurus*, finds ten words
for absence: her words
clot in stanzas, sonnets, closed rooms.

3.

When the nine-month sleep cure
didn't work, they tried hoses:
belted her with water
until out flew the truth
from every pore: how promiscuous she was
and not sorry, how she drank
thimble after thimble in the sad hours,
how she feared secrets,
wrote them all down, fell apart
with laughter down to her anklebones.
She told everything,
held nothing back after all the years
of silence, the silence
called *Composure*, as in opening a closed fan....

Now she doubles up in a lotus,
an itty-bitty at the breast,

little remora: breathe out, breathe in.
Her gulping, growing baby-girl
will soon travel out: *I have gone*
to the wildwood, mother,
don't wait up....
From mouth to mouth
the long vowels go back and forth.

Morning Coffee on Isle la Motte

I am coherently
happy now: drip coffee this lovely, windy
summer Saturday a.m. into my small, cracked
pink art-deco pot, hot milk in its
companion yellow creamer. My blue

art-deco cup
is genuine Woolworth's '36, aglow
in pre-war, post-depression glaze.
With muffins, coffee, and butter-knife
engraved Fifth Avenue Hotel (once family-

owned, and family-
thieved), I spread before me
inherited rubrics of 20th-century
commercial style. My Armenian neighbor
ambles by to bring a book on Turkish pogroms

in World War I.
The family expelled from Sivas, whipped through
desert to Aleppo. A woman grabs back her child,
gets hands sliced off like bread, like breasts,
by a Turkish scimitar. Girl raped and raped, then

still. Learn to
swallow gold rings for safekeeping; rake
them later out of your shit. Death of Mariam,
age 6, quiet, in a saddlebag. The Euphrates
filled with bodies, yet drinkable. Serop, now old,

orphaned at
the same age as my small daughter, survived
by tending sheep for local Turks; he
will not mention it for 70 years. We do,
each safe in our own diaspora, over coffee

brewed American-
style as some local boys windsurf on the lake
blowing like a scarf before us. Somewhere
in this urgent world, the terrorists are reading maps,
taking aim, replenishing their guns, but

the lawn
is empty here, wildflowered, overlong.
I don't know where my own children are:
out with their father somewhere, safely havened,
filling buckets, throwing stones at the blown scarf of lake.

The Faith-Healer

We are concerned with the apple
That falls to the ground in June,
The paraplegic, the broken child, the woman
With stenotic lungs. Not the ordinary
Atrophy of age. For that there is one cure only,
Not in our hands. We are not loquacious; in fact,
I am almost embarrassed to tell you how
Our hands are cathedrals, how the air
We breathe out vibrates like angel-wings. Yet
We sometimes succeed
Though it is no miracle, you understand, simply
Delay. We often fail. And when we fail
And the apple falls
It is not Evil, and God
Is not responsible.

Do You Take

her
him   phenobarb
scotch, weed, snow

snuff, any other
besides
from the back

or in the
usual way
like a duck

to water   naps
in the afternoon
Mademoiselle

Scientific American
umbrage
yours

with or without
ice   the
nuclear family

as the basic modality for the
preservation
of Western civ

or
romantic love
between a man and a woman

as a fragile post-
industrial phenomenon
of an overly-eroticized culture?

Mahogany

If you were a child, let's say,
lying flat on your back, lying
on a dark rug, you would see
the underside of a table, you would see
the heavy carvings of table-legs,
everything mahogany, dark; and a
chest-of-drawers, also mahogany, with its
carved handles, its ornate drawer-pulls.
Beside you, let's say, is a woman
with brown eyes and curly brown hair,
eyes and hair the color of mahogany, who
is not your mother and not your playmate, but
the kind of stranger who is supremely
your best friend (even though you never
see her again in your life) because she tells you
all the dark secrets. When she tells you
about your aunt who even in her suicide note
lied about her age, you know
with utter certainty that you, too,
will always lie about your age, and you both laugh:
she because she shouldn't have told, and you
not because you have an answer
but because now you have a question
and from now on you will always
be restless, so even when the woman

shows you what *mahogany* really means
and the best way to do it, and even if
she does it with a tongue or a hand or only
a look, you will always remember
how warm the room was, and the exact filiations
of color in that moment when everything
was mahogany and everything completely changed.

St.-Germain-des-Prés

Always it rains
and mushrooms grow in between
　　your fingers,
sprouting out of your ribs, the crook
　　of your elbow,
the hollow of your mouth: the words
　　you speak
are like the sounds of water squeezed

　　from a sponge
while you have become porous, a tissue
　　of veins. With
the thirsty narcissism of a plant
　　you adhere
to the stones, to the walls of soft
　　pumice
and, casually, a root pushes down

　　without you knowing
into the streets soft and spongy
　　as blotting paper.
Soon you never want to leave your *quartier*:
　　the desire
is to spiral in on yourself, as a vine

nods, inwardly;
you know you will never dry out,

    and, in the never-
ending rain, you crouch closer.

Each Summer

They come in over the wires, these men
from far away, sometimes transatlantically
or from Brooklyn, in their white Datsuns
or Toyotas, their voices as varied
as the times I have slept with them.
Each one has a fetching routine
I fall for: A likes to talk shop
and feeds me; B, as I recall, fancies

cutting snippets of hair. C is silent,
and D..., and so it goes.
They remind me of how dangerous
the world is, how unstable
my place in it, how even one person
can be a conquering horde. Each summer
I am overrun, jittery, looking
for trouble. You would say I am
asking for it. Each summer I let it go on:
the siege, the thrill, the battle fatigue.

What He Knew

*Isidora, a city ... where the
foreigner hesitating between two
women always encounters a third....*

—Italo Calvino, *Invisible Cities*

What he really wanted
was to slip his cashmere scarf
over her eyes, and take her from behind,
bending low over his couch. He would
watch her pleasure, darkening,
whatever of it she would allow.
He wanted her to know he torched her—
an exercise in epistemology,
if you will—and then he thought of
Marta, years ago, in Rio,
when he photographed her
sitting on the toilet, half-clothed,
twisting slightly to avoid his lens.
Her embarrassment, he liked that.
From darkness
he called out their images, hard-edged
as photos he polished carefully
each night in his studio. The places, too,
were not indistinct: Ipanema; or a hotel

in Paris, rue des Saints-Pères;
the hostel in Munich after the war;
the motel in Kew Gardens with the water bed
and mirrored ceiling. Perhaps the places
more than women, perhaps so.
The gift he gave himself, and others,
was rush of memory. What he knew?
That there is nothing more magnanimous than this world.

II

▼

Another Trashy Aubade

The sun rises, sending out
its gorgeous, polluted rays: from ten stories up
we see another day gasp to its beginning.
Ten stories. At one
hundred feet over this perilous Manhattan earth
we write to the folks back home, all is well,
we are breathing still. It is the morning
of the late twentieth century
whose Exhibit A
has trashed us into terror, its transport-
trucks and boxcars marked *meta phora*,
the transfer, from place to place.... Somewhere
a hand reaches for the throttle, the gears
engage. Yet today
we are well-
cordoned into our homes: my husband
turns his back to this dawn, the baby whimpers
briefly, and both
filled with their separate pains which mean life
return to their separate
festivities of sleep.

Ode After Nelly Sachs:
For Some Women Who Died

You who fled from him
pointlessly
or locked yourself off
motionless, expressionless, as stone
or you who joined him, slept with him,
singed by his smoke
frantic to survive

I wonder about you
across this ocean
of forty years:
so long has it taken
to see
how commonplace you were

> *as your bodies were made no longer your own*
> *as your husbands were made no longer your own*
> *as your mothers and fathers were made no longer your own*
> *as your children were made no longer your own*

as your children...
who looked to you in wonder
(once kept tight as almonds
within you)
were turned to smoke
and dust. On that journey

in that mid-century whirr
when a race was turned to smoke
in the momentary jarring of a solstice
I, too, might have traveled
burned—
another pulsing
of an extinguished star.

Planting Children: 1939

Oh quick, garner the children.
Stash them in baskets, egg crates,
dresser drawers, anywhere;
kiss their thin necks in the hollow
where the blood pulses,
kiss their warm ears. The train already
is raising dust,
the lists are drawn up, the cows
no longer look up from pasture.
It is the iron hinge, the parting.
Now, quick, shove the babies underground
like spuds: let them root there
for forty years, let them
come up storytellers, all eyes.

On Hearing That Childbirth Is Like Orgasm

So, maybe it's not a maiming
altogether
but some weird daylong fairy tale

as the door opens into a new chateau
and the moat closes over
behind you. It's magic:
like pricking your finger, the pin
just some new animal, for your pleasure;
a kind of tickle, you don't feel it

anyway
having gone somewhere beyond
pain, your
body limp and blooming as an anemone, O
the lush stories to tell! the extravagance! the irresistible
rules! to be
strapped to stirrups, your wrists
chained.... Classier even than *The Story of O*
it's what the good fairy promised

and the good girls get:
the kiss in the turret, the happy-ever-after.

Breathing

I used to hover
at the ribs of my daughter's crib
resting my hand
on the rise/fall of her chest,
quickening like a bird's.

Later I started
listening to my husband,
to each time he lost—and caught—
his breath.
I became the landlord of breathing

and know its grammar:
its assertions and longing, its
crocus-shape, its radical
hesitations.
Now there are two daughters,
the same husband, all
breathing, all somehow
making it to morning.

Still I attend these quilted
nightly monologues:
I cannot yet
breathe easy.

Lilly's Song

I hold my daughter up to the fire-
light: tiny blossom, perfect snail
whose heart blooms
in her like springtime, opening
and opening. The morsels of her cry
bend us in, saying *I*, *I*,
I'm arrived! and we curl around her
like fingers, weaving lullabies.
All the world's
hers now, her nest warm as desire
while her father croons over her:
My lover, he sings,
My lover, childbride.

The Idea of Roads
at Gondreville-la-Franche

Roads have their own talk
as bones do—
oblivious to angers,
uprisings, love affairs

they perambulate
like slow eels
or fan out in spokes;
join, couple, with no

restraints of number.
They are simple—
with the mystery of algebra.
They speak an arcane grammar

common to the overlooked,
the fool. Neither morbid
nor ethical, their thoughts
are more like recipes:

if you go out at night
you can hear them
calibrating to each other
across the fields.

Nervus Erotis

That after all the hot days' glow
Not one night belongs to us....
The tuberoses take on the color of my blood
Flickering flame-like from their calyxes.

Tell me at night if your soul also cries
Leaping frightened from sleep
Like the night-shriek of birds in the wild.

The whole world shines red
As though life bled soul-wide;
My heart hungers, starved.
Death stares out from its red ghost-eye.

Tell me at night if your soul also mourns
Flooded by the strong tuberoses' odor
As it gnaws on the nerve of the florid dream.

(after Else Lasker-Schüler)

Talk, You

I like talking with you, simply that:
conversing, a turning-with or -around, as in
your turning around to face me
suddenly, saying *Come*, and I turn
with you, for a sometime
hand under my under-
things, and you telling me
what you would do, where,
on what part of my body
you might talk to me differently.
At your turning,
each part of my body turns to verb.
We are the opposite of
tongue-tied, if there were such an
antonym; we are synonyms
for limbs' loosening of syntax,
and yet turn to nothing: *It's just talk.*

Postcard from Idyllic
Isle la Motte

Here in Isle la Motte, summer
'81, daisies dot the grass, pink
hollyhocks lean drunkenly. It is
midday's needlepoint of stillness
with children cooped and
napping behind screens. Latticed

in my *chaise*, lemonaded,
I suddenly see myself at eight
in Provincetown: some strange child
has met us at the door with
curtsies, grown-ups humming
in the background, and there's
my father, somewhat drunk, sliding

from the woods on his eminent,
legal rear. It must be '51
and cocktails: all the other
guests seem not to notice, lean
like hollyhocks as the
Provincetown summer rolls on, lush
and undisturbed. In gusts
of memory, sunned, silent, I wait
for my own child's
wild, psychotic, post-nap cry.

In Heat

The grasses whiten, the powerful gulls
return to the lake, having tasted the bleached
upturned lips of a ploughed field.
I, too, wear white. I would come

at noon, pressing my wrist
to the forehead of all your fevers
as the face of the sun curves against us
like another bone. Now the June-lilies

open their burnished faces, lake and fields
lie open to the white discs of gulls.
You are tossing, now, tossing:
the air flashes around you its whitened dust.

Dark and Nameless

When the girl raises
her white gauze skirt
to show her left hip grazed
by a bullet, the man
from the news agency
shoots her again, 13 and
sober as an icon.
The young boy to her side
stares into the shutter
as if it could help.
All the fathers

in their muddy village have just
been shot. The photographer
saw the collage of bodies,
the ditch, the tree
splashed with blood. Up goes gauze
over hip thin as a grain
of rice, he shoots, the boy
stares, a direct hit.
She claims one of the dead fathers.
His claim is dark and
nameless as the mud he will
always live in.

She Wakes Up

Last act. Everyone is dead, bones
piled up like Cambodia. Enter the Prince
waving his arms: *Ahhh*, he says,
there's a lotta garbage around here.
But the Lilac Fairy has saved the day:
Sleeping Beauty is not dead, that luscious girl,
only snoozing a hundred years.
There she is, on a bier, her ten toes
pointing to the sky, like a dead mouse.
Wait! He has kissed her, and everyone
wakes up. Mommy! Daddy! A hundred years later
and they're still in love.

It doesn't matter
she hasn't read a thing in years;
the Prince can fill her in. They rub a bit
like cats while he tells her
what of the century she's missed: trench warfare,
pogroms, mass graves, the names
of all the camps. They settle down
to nuzzle. *Touch me*, she says,
You do me, I'll do you.

Playground

Lilly's my jungle-gym junkie: at two
she swings, blonde and simian,
bar to bar, while Kate, the baby,
queens it in the sand. Poland, Pakistan,

Yugoslavia, Greece: their well-known
banal histories have sent their kids
to play with mine, cut the cord of mother-
tongue, and flung them out

like gloves, the emigré-toddler set.
My requests can be ignored
in several languages: I am polyglot
but sandbagged where Ivan, little Tito,

has climbed on me with dirty sneaks.
Who's got an extra diaper, who makes
only ten thou a year? How
do they do it and still dress

Isidora from Saks Fifth?
And where do we send them later on: to
learn Hebrew at Ramaz, French
at the lycée, or to get the best

at Brearley? Can any kid
survive at P.S. 75? Kate,
newly upright, beams joy to me
from her nest of sand, my coffee's

cold, Lilly's drink is warm, and our
best-dressed, fluent, dirty children
make the best of
such totalitarian love.

III

▼

Dead, Dinner, or Naked

I. Adam and Eve in the Blue Ridge Mountains

Dinner first: some blue-plate special
buzz of Gallo
garden-variety plastic ferns, the weight
of his eyes on her
the snake out of his tree

later they will deflower each other
slightly potted
illegally locked
in a floral motel room
(ersatz colonial)
in the Blue Ridge
the blue heaviness of the mountains
blue mists around the trees

though hardly great, or even good
she is book-perfect:
weeping a lot
blue-blooded, a little broken

II. Later, at a Bar in Gramercy Park

Beyond worn-out
they drank California

while she lay on him
all her ancestry
branched and heavy as candelabra

and he so light
so, even now, without history

between trips to the ladies' room
she told him marvelous drivel
scandal
saying, each time,
don't listen
you shouldn't have to hear this

wide as a shot of Halcion
wide as a freeway
he listened, prelapsarian,
still thinking he would live forever

III. Much Later, Adam Dreams of Two Women

There is something about him
both twisted and lyrical:
quasi-alcoholic, insomniac, hearing music
in the scrapings of steel

there he is, in bed,
Eve on one hand, a beer in the other,
and *Blue Velvet* on the VCR;
he would be thinking
of some other woman, if there were one,
wondering

what she would do, if
or he is dreaming
into the future of Abraham
having it both ways
with Sarah and Hagar

Adam's sin is even now millennia-old:
he could make love
to one while imagining another—
he wants to be clear of the Garden
to fall and be tortured forever

IV. The Forevers

From the fall
of the 2nd Temple to the camps
from the Milvian Bridge
to the camps, from cuneiform
and cunnilingus, starfish
and star wars, from haiku
and terza rima, it is always
goodbye, goodbye, snaking out
of the garden, as if
there were an out, as if
there were anything but dead, dinner, or naked

Wintering

Everything as usual: November
and the gray stones of the church
flattening in the pale winter light.
Boys and girls pull on the little mittens
we have clamped to their sleeves
and come home early, calling for supper,
while in some chilly field
a pony grazes on late apples. Light
peels away like mica: snow
is about to erase another season.
And in some season, themselves having wintered,
our children, if all goes well,
will watch us die, and go on.

Square Laurent Prache

Let's sit here upon the bench:
     strange, tense,
expectant as travelers walled
     in a formal garden

where you in all freedom
     cup your hand
softly to my throat; where you touch
     with a gloved

soft stroke, claiming old gestures
     already shared,
ornate secrets told before, while plump
     Guillaume Apollinaire

watches blankly with the endless intact
     stare Picasso
gave him, the garden's totem—
     and the sun!

the sun unfurls itself striated through
     foliage of linden:
trees dark, thick, webbed as maidenbush,
     punctured

all over with linden-cones:
        some white, others
an older, bloodier pink; and who knows
        what colors, what

dreams, what new angles
        of pleasure
the quick, intransigent night will
        drown us in?

City Blizzard

From Morningside Heights down,
up, wherever you look, the gray
sky settles like martial law,
its syntax
falling on stalled
cars, pedestrians, children's
ready tongues.
Broadway buses, slow and non-
partisan, nose through
under my window, heavy
with pleated snow.
Our city,
no longer gridded
or vertical, flattens
and stretches sideways
like the candid palm of a mitten:
its murderous
codicils erased by snow's
clean impartial verdict.

Just Another Love Affair

In the ordinary way of summer
she was clover-languid   sybaritic
he from another town   he from
another strain   Both
wore white overalls   à la mode
believing themselves   untouched
by culture   tasting upon each other
soy flour   sea salt and honey
like fresh bread   rising
though the fragrant simile
is inexact: neither, in those moments,
cared for commodities   nor the so-called

domestic virtues   It was all love
in the dunes by day   and at nights
chiming of crystal   Both slept well
not awakened   by babies, nor breaking
of glass   thinking it was the truth
of each other   each was after,
licking each other's alphabet
from A to Z and back   and calling out
all the golden names   In other words
theirs was indistinguishable
from many such loves   and not without
disaster   for all that

The Park, at Midnight

Late May. You can stand under lilacs
and be drenched:
what I knew
when I ran away there, to "under the lilacs,"
holding my paper bag of provisions—
two slices of rye bread, rubbed with garlic,
a meal-in-the-desert. Pure fragrance, a feast.
Years later, running away again,

and further,
I said *yes* when someone called me *Catherine*,
followed him to 42nd Street, into
the movies, more cavernous and fragrant
than rye-and-garlic, sweeter than lilacs,
where the giant screen blazed with a man
closer than neon
leaning over a pool table, a crazed look in his eyes;

while my new love, my stranger,
leaned over me, taking my hand,
saying *hold it, go down on it.*
Where could I go but down? Home,
of all places?
No, said the stranger, said the man

on the screen lining up the ball. Remember
the wild taste of garlic, the smell of lilacs:

escape now to the park, at midnight,
to consort
with the benign local rapists and addicts,
the young men
in leather jackets, throwing sticks in long arcs
for their dogs in the dense midnight light.
The dogs fetch and return,
run away and come back, obeying some instinct,

some compulsion: like losing love, finding it,
only to ask to lose it again.

Scripture

*So I opened my mouth and he gave me
the scroll to eat....Then I ate it, and it
was in my mouth as sweet as honey.*

—Ezekiel, 3:2-3

She lives his words. Everything
he says comes true. Call it
a new invasion: flush
of language, a beachhead
he never thought
to take before. *What's the drill?*
he asks, and
drills her to the bed, drilling her
all the while
in tea-party good manners.
Say please and thank you.
She says please, please,
a hundred-times please
but forgets the thanks, because
neither has a shred
of language now.
She's swallowed all his words.

Alone, Without an Angel

Torrents of traffic
flood Amsterdam Avenue: winds

push people against walls.
Carnage at every corner, streets

I used to be familiar with
full of shattered windshields, the motor

all over the pavement, sonnets
of sirens. But this is not real,

don't worry, it is only metaphor:
a kind of neurosis, another

risky way of saying
"alone, without an angel."

Try again: try to "remember"
as if you witnessed it, or authored it, how

in some other place,
not here, in this city,

an angel spread its wings
like floodlights—a dim theology that

not here, but somewhere,
an angel traffics with this world.

Burn

for Jean-François

(1980-88)

1.

Burning images
of the long-hot:

route 129
already blasted at 10 a.m.
chicory

in road-edge spondees
pale blue
heat bleached

dry grasses
and St. Anne's Shrine
rising in its white

godly A-frame
joual prayers
my bicycle chain

scraping
in iambs
against the gears

2.

my daughter
with a hoofprint
branded on her back

where the yearling
reared
and grazed her

is disconnected
from her fear, still yearns
for horses—

the soft burn of them
under her thighs
in cantering dactyls

3.

and Jean-François
summer '88
at 8-plus years

his body
enjambed
across telephone wires

flung there
by a car passing Iberville
at 80 k

is disconnected
his brain
having burst

like a wildflower
gone heatedly
to seed

4.

Cadence
of midmorning outdoor mass
fans out

to the sky, over lake
its alexandrines
gathered

by the God of shining black-top
of cars
with jet exhaust

of hot heather and pale goldenrod
of drought
of a child burned out

who died in a heat wave
that, his last summer,
seemed to have

no relief, no end

Telling Her

for J. M. N.

(1916-84)

My best, best, most special
dreamt herself into a pit of nightmare and
could not return to sleep, so I said, Yes,
yes, I also had those dreams
and never forgot. The intruder
on the porch was one, the fire was another;
a third even now
I cannot tell. Now more lately the dream is
of my mother calling me,
reciting numbers in a strange voice,
while I plead Mother, *mother*,
speak up, and then she dies
in some other dream, a few days later.
Now I find myself leaping to talk to her.
There is not one day goes by, sometimes
I feel not one moment, without
that desperate urge to tell a story,
some little anecdote, or just to say
something totally innocuous, but full
of my affection, like, *Well*,
did you wear your mittens out today? or
Oh, is the dryer fixed? or *You'll never*

guess who called! Not to make up
for all those years of silence, which weren't
very silent anyway, but to keep her
tied to me with that remarkable elastic
bond that winds its way now
down into another generation,
my best, best, most special ones,
stilled by their own stiff, childhood silence,
while my dream is telling, always
the dream is telling her, always trying to tell.

Front Porch

1.

When the curtain opens
on a front porch, says the critic,
I walk out, meaning,
I suppose, those ubiquitous
rocking-chairs, an old grand-
pa or ma, the usual cataclysm
of ho-hum raw emotion,
plenitude of gnats, fireflies, and
wisteria at dusk.
Let me not omit
from this banned semiology
of porches, my own front porch
on the Maryland corner
of First and Anson, almost blotted out
by a scrim of rhododendrons
fanged with pink blooms.
This front porch is where

the featureless intruder
stands in my nightmare
peering through windows, searching
for me like a magnet. Where
I lay in a chaise-longue one hot day
in '55, and Jesse

Something-or-other,
fearless, faceless,
squashed his blonde face
against mine and kissed me
full on the mouth, full
of the blonde smell of the intruder
and I bolted up, alien, compromised,
having suddenly conceived.

2.

Even worse, the critic continues,
someone's mother always has cancer. It's true
my mother does have cancer,
it's a cliché, a convention, you can hardly
blame her. Probably
I have cancer too, almost certainly;
perhaps it has already leaked down,
down to my daughters, killing
each other so innocently there on the porch.

Perhaps the clear scrim of blood
is already transformed, the understudies
already warmed up
and taking over. Perhaps in my play
my children will be orphans, almost certainly
I will be an orphan, a tree will fall
on my car, the plane will crash, the gun
will go off, we will lose everything, we will
have to emigrate, we will be jammed

into boxcars, there will be no water, someone
with insignias will meet us, another pogrom
is waiting in the wings. Surely
this is my front porch for life.

Notes

The quotation in "The Faith-Healer" is from the *New York Times*.

The title, "Alone, Without an Angel" is from "Something Personal" by Haim Gouri.